You've Got This!

The Fempreneur Guide To Finally Believing You're Enough So You Can Build A Business That You Love, Find The Success That You Deserve And Create A Life Without Limits

~

A book by: Gemma James

Foreword by: Tesa Colvin, TV Show Host, Bestselling Author, and Award Winning Publishing Consultant

Copyright

You Got This!

The Fempreneur Guide to Finally Believing You're Enough So You Can Build a Business That You Love, Find the Success that You Deserve and Create a Life Without Limits

~Dedication~

For my Husband, Gareth, for always allowing me to be 100% 'me'.

For my Mum - I did it Mum! Thank you for always believing I would.

And for my incredible daughter, Cerys. For always believing I'm perfect even when I don't see it myself. I want to give you the World my darling girl, but it's already yours for the taking. There are so many limitless possibilities out there for you, never let anyone dull your sparkle!

Table of Content

~Acknowledgements~

My heart is full of gratitude as I sit here writing the Acknowledgments for this book. There are so many people I want to thank but I'll keep it short and sweet (like me!). Firstly, this book would still be a dream in my head if it wasn't for the amazing support of Tesa Colvin, Publishing Consultant Extraordinaire! Thank you Tesa for helping me get the words out, for helping me to find my voice and for reminding me, constantly, that it's a conversation! I'm still astounded that I wrote this book in 7 weeks and grateful doesn't even come close to how I feel about you!

Thanks also go to my amazing Tribe of Dream Life Creators, my fabulous Community, clients, customers and Dream Life Project Members. Your continued support, excitement and trust in me inspires me every day. I trust this book will inspire you too and just know that I had some of you in mind in particular when I wrote this book!

My Biz Besties (you know who you are), I am blessed to have you in my circle, I am grateful for you every day and you motivate me to keep pushing forward. Everything Always Works Out For Us right?

And finally my wonderful family. For not really understanding what I do but supporting it anyway!

Love to you all xxx

~Foreword~

"Enoughness" is something we all struggle with.

More often than not, we work overtime trying to cover this feeling of inadequacy. Our efforts are mostly dedicated to hiding the cracks in the facades we have established over time, but we never deal with the root.

In my time as a Coach and Consultant I have spent the majority of time helping my clients believe they were worth their dreams and goals. It was often a tug of war between what they hoped and wished for and that nagging feeling deep within them that said that they were not good enough to realize such dreams.

Watching this happen time and time again in my own life and with the people I supported was heartbreaking, frustrating, and of course, it made the path to reaching those goals longer and harder than necessary.

But now, thanks to Author Gemma James, who pulls back the curtain on her own battle with "enoughness", we can do the real (no B.S.) work needed to end the habitual cycles of self-talk that have held us back for far too long.

Get ready to go on a journey that strengthens you, changes the trajectory of your life AND does the same for those looking up to you and waiting to walk in your footsteps.

~**Tesa Colvin**~

TV Show Host, Bestselling Author, and Award Winning Publishing Consultant

Chapter 1

FIVE YEAR OLD DECISIONS AND STONE WASH JEANS...

I now know the exact moment I decided I wasn't good enough.

I was standing at the bottom of the stairs. Wearing stonewash jeans and an awful green shell suit jacket (apparently it was fashionable back then). I was five years old. My dad was standing in the doorway of our open front door, suitcase in hand. I was crying, my mum was crying, I think my brother was crying. And I had no idea why.

I don't remember the exact words he said but let's just say that he was leaving and wouldn't be coming back. I didn't get it. I was confused and sad and assumed, in my five year old mind, that I must have done something wrong. That I'd been bad and that was why my dad didn't want to stick around. Maybe if I'd listened better, or slept in longer or picked up my Care Bears from the floor.

Whatever I'd done, it hadn't been enough.

That's what my five year old brain had chosen to decide. Because I didn't know any different.

What I wouldn't know until much, much later was that the decision I made that day at the bottom of the stairs in my horrid green shell suit jacket, impacted so much of my life into my early 30s. So many situations, events, decisions and choices.

Like the time I was bullied in school for three whole years. Because I was short and wore glasses and got good grades (so basically I stood out like a sore thumb). I went from loving school and having really close friends, to dreading it every day, crying in the toilets and feeling so incredibly alone. What did I decide?

That I wasn't enough.

I wasn't tall enough or pretty enough or popular enough….or stupid enough?! Yeah, I actually remember wishing I wasn't so clever and didn't get such good marks for my homework so that the bullies would like me and accept me. To the point where I stopped actually 'trying' so hard and let my grades slip so that maybe, just maybe, I'd be accepted.

And like the time an ex-boyfriend said to me in the car on the way home from the movies that he'd consider marrying me if I 'lost a bit of weight and sorted myself out a bit'. Yeah. Asshole. What did I decide?

That I wasn't enough.

I wasn't thin enough or attractive enough or 'good' enough.

(I also decided fairly soon after, that we weren't 'meant to be' and I ended things, thank goodness! But that's a different story for another time…)

But in the moment I decided that I wasn't good enough.

And like the time I became a mother. I gave birth to the most beautiful amazing wonderful little girl who fills my heart with joy every single day but in the first few months of her life I felt like a failure regularly. Because the birth hadn't gone as planned, because I wasn't able to breastfeed, because I wasn't able to hold her the moment she was born as I was so out of it. Because I didn't get the overwhelming surge of love the minute she was born that the movies tell you about and instead didn't feel it until two days later. If you're a mum then I'm sure you've felt it #mumguilt

But this just added to the belief that had already been established in my brain. At this point it had taken up residence, signed the papers and moved the furniture.

This just confirmed what I already knew to be true.

I wasn't good enough.

It was almost like every time something sucky happened I'd think 'well obviously that happened, because I'm not good enough! Why did I expect anything else?'

And then something happened that changed my entire world as I understood it. I learned about our brains, how habits and beliefs are formed and I discovered the world of the Law of Attraction and having a positive and successful mindset.

I became open to new possibilities.

I CHOSE to decide new things. I CHOSE to learn some new things. I CHOSE to no longer live an 'ordinary' life. I CHOSE TO BE EXTRAORDINARY.

But of course, this didn't happen overnight.

There were several steps I put in place before I got there.

And that's what I'm sharing with you within the pages of this book. I'll be explaining WHY you feel a certain way sometimes, how your beliefs are formed and the limitations these put on you. And then I'll be giving you some techniques and steps you can take to not only understand them but change them.

So you can get there too.

Are you ready to feel like you deserve it? Are you ready to feel good enough?

Are you ready to be extraordinary?

Then let's dive in.

Chapter 2

THE 7 YEAR OLD WHO RULES YOUR LIFE.

'We learn our belief systems as very little children, and then we move through life creating experiences to match our beliefs.' -Louise L. Hay

My Dad left because I'm not good enough. I should have been better behaved, nicer, smarter, prettier, funnier. If I was good enough he wouldn't have left.

That's what I decided on that day when I was five years old and my Dad left the house with his suitcase in hand. I know NOW of course that my not being good enough had nothing to do with it, and my belief about not being good enough was never backed up by my mum or my brother - it's not like they ever said 'this is all your fault, if you'd been better he would have stayed' but in my five year old mind - with no real knowledge about relationships and love and family and arguments and the way the world works sometimes, this is what I decided.

What you say to yourself means EVERYTHING. I could tell you you're amazing until the cows come home but until YOU believe it, nothing's going to change.

But for you to REALLY start believing you're worthy of your dreams and you're more than good enough just as you are, it's important for you to understand why you have such debilitating crappy limiting thoughts about not being good enough in the first place.

It all starts as children. As our bodies are developing so are our brains. I don't want to get too technical and 'sciencey' here because it's not important for the purposes of your transformation but I do want to touch on it because when you know WHY, you know HOW you can change it.

Here's the thing - you're not special.

Don't get me wrong, you're totally awesome and you're unique in your DNA and you have the real power to be extraordinary - you can be, do and have whatever you want. You're clever and funny and beautiful inside and out and you're worthy of creating your ultimate Dream Life....

But you're not special.

Because we all - EVERY SINGLE ONE OF US - has limiting beliefs and doubts and fears. It's how we're wired. It's how our brains work in order to keep us safe. That's its only job. To protect you from anything that may cause you pain. It doesn't know the difference between a pain that may cause you emotional harm - like the words of a school bully who made you want to hide in your bedroom - and actual real significant danger - like being chased by a pack of wolves. It literally picks up on anything that may feel a little uncomfortable and it goes into flight or fight mode to keep you safe.

You may also know this referred to as your 'comfort zone'.

So how is this comfort zone built?

It starts when we're very young. We build up these walls around us based on everything we hear, see, witness. From things our parents say, our teachers say, our friends, society, media, religion then later in life through our bosses, relationships and so on.

Because we don't know any different at this age, we're like little sponges absorbing everything around us - our brains just take it as fact. It will then use these 'facts' (aka your beliefs) to help us as we go about our life. Reminding us of them when we're faced with a situation that might 'harm us' because it goes against our beliefs.

For example, if you were brought up in a household where you were constantly told that only greedy people are rich and it's more humble to be poor, that you're a nicer person if you're poor, then in your later life when you're met with a situation to make some real good money, your brain is going to go 'hang on, you believe that only greedy people are rich and you don't want to be greedy, you want to be a nice person' and so it will do everything in its power to prevent you from harm (i.e. never let you be rich so you're not greedy).

It will do this by subconsciously reminding you of times when you were told that it's nicer to be poor, remind you of people you met who were perhaps not the nicest people but they had a lot of money (confirming your belief that rich people are assholes), will send stress chemicals around your body when you're faced with a situation where you could potentially make more money - let's say the chance to take on a big client in your business, or receive a promotion with a big pay rise at work - so your palms sweat and you get a sick feeling in your stomach and you doubt your abilities and so tell yourself that you don't really want it anyway.

So you don't win the client or you don't get the promotion and the subconscious part of your brain sits back looking all smug, feeling all proud of itself for keeping you safe and doing its job so wonderfully. And you stay within your comfort zone a little longer.

The things we hear and see and are subject to when we are young sow the seeds for these beliefs to form. It's not like if someone says something once then you're going to suddenly have a belief around it but if you're hearing it over and over again for example, your brain will then start to use these words and thoughts and situations as evidence for why you can and can't, should or shouldn't do something. All in an attempt to keep you safe, secure and happy.

Media has a lot to answer for in this respect. I notice this a lot more now since I've become aware of how our beliefs are formed and have a much different perception of money than I had growing up. I watch so many movies now that just make me cringe. They're usually chick flicks or family type movies where there's a girl and a love interest. She thinks she wants the one in the suit with lots of money for example but he turns out to be a cheating asshole and so instead falls in love with the humble store assistant who doesn't have any money but treats her like a princess (because you're nice when you're poor and an asshole when you're rich right?). That sounds like a lame movie I know but you get the idea. And I bet you can think of a movie now where a similar situation has happened - with a similar message: Don't be rich or you'll end up a friendless asshole.

So why have I called this chapter 'The 7 Year Old Who Rules Your Life?'

Because so much of what we take in when we're young affects so much of what we do when we're older. It directs the decisions we make, the things we do, the goals and dreams we go after and the ones we shy away from. The people we associate with and what we feel we 'deserve'.

I decided when I was five that I wasn't good enough. This belief was deeper rooted when I was bullied at school because I felt like I didn't fit in. It went deeper still when my first ever boyfriend dumped me over the phone in front of his friends (I was 12 and we'd been 'going out' for three months. I thought I'd never recover and I'd be alone forever…). This belief went deeper when I discovered another boyfriend had cheated on me and then broke up with me because he liked the other girl more (I was 19 at this time so it stung a little bit more). The belief went deeper when another boyfriend told me he'd consider marrying me if I lost a bit of weight and 'sorted myself out a bit'. There's a bit of a theme arising here isn't there…

All of these situations and relationships meant that I had some serious self-limiting beliefs and doubts about my worth. Always questioning whether I was good enough. Worrying that people were talking about me behind my back (and assuming they were because I wasn't 'cool enough' or 'popular enough' or 'pretty enough'), not sticking up for myself or expressing my own opinion. I'd agree with everyone because I was worried about what they would think otherwise. I'd sit in meetings at work but I'd never speak up or offer suggestions because I assumed they'd think they were stupid ideas, even though someone else would have a very similar idea and was praised wonderfully for it, and I'd then beat myself up for NOT speaking up and feeling envious of the other person because it was my idea first and....round and round it went.

And when it came to my business? Oh my goodness! Fear, doubt, no confidence, no clarity, no focus. I spent so much time doing what I thought I 'should' do, watching what others were doing and trying to do the same but then wondering why it didn't work. I had no confidence in my own ideas and so didn't stick with any of them, choosing 'shiny object syndrome' instead.

If you're reading this book then there's a strong chance that you can resonate with this.

Now, you may not have had a traumatic experience at such a young age like a parent leaving when you were five but I can guarantee that the things you heard and saw and felt when growing up have influenced where you are today.

Think back throughout your life to times when you've not felt good enough. Think about things you've heard, people you've met, events and situations where your confidence was crushed. Think about your early childhood and your life growing up in your home, think about school and teachers you had, friends you had, any times that you were bullied or failed in class, think about the jobs you've held and how you felt there. Spend some time on this, the longer you do this the more you'll spark your subconscious memories and the more will come up for you.

This isn't to make you feel crap about all the sucky things that have happened in your life but more so you can start to be aware of where your limiting beliefs about not being good enough have come from.

This may take much deeper digging through techniques like hypnotherapy but it's likely a few things will come up for you just by sitting down and thinking about it. When you have this clarity of where your beliefs have come from or have shown up in your life, you can start to take the steps to change them.

I give you some tools and techniques at the end of this book that you can use to start uncovering some of your limiting beliefs so you can have a better understanding of where they come from. It will be personal for everyone. We all have these crappy limiting beliefs about not being good enough but for some that's about not HAVING enough, for some it's not BEING enough, for some it's not DOING enough. And for some it's a combination of all 3 and some others thrown in for good measure.

Start by thinking about some of the things you heard regularly growing up - most likely from your parents and other close members of your family or perhaps your teachers at school. What things do you find yourself saying now that you remember your parents saying to you when you were a child?

I asked the members of my Dream Life Creators Club this very question and here are some of their responses - you may recognize some from your own childhood.

'We're just not that lucky.'

'Keep an eye on it because you'll never get your arse in it!' (in relation to a car)

'Wanting too much money is greedy.'

'Money doesn't grow on trees.'

'It's alright for some!'

'How the other half live.'

'Don't be selfish.'

'Don't be stupid.'

'You don't need that.'

'They have more money than they know what to do with.'

'Money goes to money.'

'You won't get anywhere unless you work hard.'

'There are two ways to get money - hard work and dishonesty.'

'You spend money like it's water.'

'The bills won't pay themselves.'

'If you want it you have to earn it.'

'Work hard, play hard.'

'Do I look like a bank?'

'You have to have the bad days to realise the good days.'

'Don't be greedy.'

And here are some from my own childhood:

'If it seems too good to be true it probably is.'

'You can't have your cake and eat it'

'A job isn't something that regular people love, that's only in the movies. You go to work so you can afford nice things.'

'You're not good at math and science and those kinds of subjects, you should stick to English Literature and languages.' (that one was from a teacher when I was about 12 which gave me the belief that I wasn't good at math so I didn't even bother trying as I was going to fail anyway right? It turns out that I'm actually not as crap at math as I thought…)

Now it's your turn. Note down those things that you remember from your childhood and start to think about some of the times they may have held you back.

Chapter 3

FALSE EVIDENCE APPEARING REAL

'I am an old man and have known a great many troubles....but most of them never happened' - Mark Twain

'Who here in this room has a fear about not being good enough?' Tony asks.

'That's me all over!' I say in my head as I tentatively raise my hand. And then I remember holding my breath as I saw hand after hand after hand being raised into the air. Each person with a look on their face of 'how does he know that?' I was standing in the middle of an arena in London on Day 1 of a 4 day Tony Robbins transformational seminar. 10,000 people from over 60 countries - all races, religions, beliefs, sexes, ages. And at least 90% of the people had their hand in the air when Tony asked that question. Suddenly, I felt much less alone.

It turns out that a fear of not being good enough is one of the most common fears a person has. It even has its own name - Atelophobia.

When I asked the members of my free Community 'The Dream Life Creators Club' if they had ever had a fear of not being good enough I was met with a resounding Yes. 100% of the people who responded said they felt they weren't good enough, some 'all the time'. They were scared of not succeeding in their business or losing it all and having to find other work, wondering why people would listen to them and suffering with 'imposter syndrome'.

So if you're feeling this way I can guarantee you're absolutely not alone.

But where does this fear come from? It all stems back to your beliefs and that 7 year old version of you from Chapter 2. Remember your brain just wants to keep you safe. That is its only job. So the habits and beliefs that have been programmed into your brain is what is used to keep you within the walls of your comfort zone. Nice and safe…. And ordinary…

So anytime you start to push the walls of these comfort zones your brain is going to do everything in its power to stop you from doing it so that you stay where it's comfortable and safe.

Let's say for example that you have been given the opportunity to give a talk on stage in front of a room full of people. This is a fantastic opportunity for your business; you know you could build rapport and connections with more people and generate some income from it that will help your success grow. But you feel a bit nervous about it as you've never done it before and you don't want to look stupid. Your brain picks up on these nervous signals and thinks you must be in real danger (as it doesn't know the difference right?) and so it starts to respond by sending stress chemicals around your body to help you either fight or run away, your body then responds by giving you a sick feeling in your stomach, maybe your palms start to sweat. Then your subconscious goes into overdrive and starts to bring up all this shit from your life - suddenly you're remembering when you were 11 and you had to give a presentation in Assembly and you were so scared that you vomited all over the stage and all the kids laughed. And the time you were 15 collecting an award and you tripped up the steps onto the stage and fell on your face. And the time when you were called upon in a meeting for an idea but were shut down by the boss and made to feel about 5 inches tall...

All in an attempt to make you 'give in' and not go for it so you're not subjected to any potential harm.

That, in a nutshell, is what Fear is. False Evidence Appearing Real. You don't know that if you accept the speaking opportunity that you'll vomit all over the stage or fall flat on your face but in the moment, it all now feels very real. You can only see the potential negatives and so choose instead to stay where it's comfortable.

Improving your confidence and self-belief (and as a result generating more abundance and success) is not about being 'fearless' - you'll still have fears come up, that's just how your brain works - but it's about how you deal with it. A wonderful mentor and friend of mine once said to me 'How you face your fears will determine your success. Will you Face Everything And Run or Face Everything And Rise?' I loved that and it stays with me today.

I choose to RISE.

And I want you to do the same.

I encourage you to keep a Success Journal. Start today. Grab a brand new journal or notebook (this doesn't have to be an expensive one, you can find some pretty ones in your local discount store I'm sure). Then use this journal to write down ALL of your wins. Every. Single. One.

If somebody left you a nice review or testimonial on your Facebook Page - note it down.
If somebody gave you a compliment, either online or in person - note it down.
If you secured a new client, made another sale or got to 1000 followers on Instagram - note it down.
If you had your first 1k month - note it down.

Note down what happened, when and how it made you feel.

It might look a little something like this:

February 13th

Lisa Smith commented on my Facebook post today that my Valentine's Wax Melts were beautiful and she loved the packaging! That makes me feel awesome and super proud!

However big or small you feel the 'win' is, write it down in your Success Journal. The more you acknowledge the small wins, the quicker the bigger wins will follow.

Then whenever you have doubts or fears arise, whenever you feel your belief wavering and you wonder if you're good enough, whenever you ask yourself if it's really possible for you and who would listen to you and what's so great about you and all the other crap we come up with to stop ourselves from stepping up - read through your Success Journal. Remind yourself of how awesome you are, of everything you've accomplished, of how far you've come.

Then own your awesome self, hold your head high.

Face Everything And RISE! You've got this.

Chapter 4

LET IT GO

"Your constant positive posts are exhausting!" a 'friend' said to me a few years ago, in response to me sharing inspirational quotes, motivational videos and other positive encouraging posts on my social media. Sure, I was trying to build a business, to generate income so I could leave my job that left me feeling undervalued and unfulfilled, but I was also trying to share a daily message of positivity, gratitude and self-belief as I was starting to understand about the importance of having a success mindset.

But my friend's response to that was to find it exhausting.

Why?

Because we're brought up in a society where it's more 'normal' to complain, to talk about the mundane, to share the trivial parts of our lives on social media sharing what we're having for dinner that night or complaining that it's Monday AGAIN and it's raining AGAIN. So that it's weird and unusual and 'exhausting' when someone tries to break away from the norm and share something positive.

So instead we go about our days (and I used to be included in this 'we' class) living a life of quiet desperation. Feeling stuck in a rut, complaining and moaning about trivial things, focusing on what's lacking from our lives and generally just plodding through life.

In this chapter I'm going to talk about something that will go against that norm. You may feel uncomfortable, you may not think this is relevant to you or perhaps is something you can 'put off for now' but I strongly urge you to take serious note of the message in this chapter.

I'm talking about the power of letting go. Letting go of negative people and influences in your life.

Why?

Because if you REALLY want to feel good enough to run your business, feel worthy of your dreams and goals, and truly feel like you deserve to have massive success? Then you need to be surrounding yourself with people who know you are, can and do too.

If you really want to gain more confidence, believe in the awesome being that you already are and achieve way more success than you ever thought possible then you won't want to miss this chapter.

This was a tough one for me to come to terms with at first and it took me a while to really get on board with it. Saying things like 'I'm sure this isn't ACTUALLY true', 'I don't see how this ACTUALLY helps you become more successful' and my favourite 'I think my situation is a bit different and this is for other people...'

All of these excuses, and many others like it, were just covering up the fact that I was scared shitless.

Scared of losing people from my life and regretting it.

Scared of being more 'me' and people not liking it.

Scared of offending people.

Scared of letting people down.

Scared of doing/saying/being the 'wrong' thing.

Scared that the grass wouldn't be 'greener on the other side'.

Scared that I'd make declarations and then fail.

Scared that people would call me out on my fear and doubt.

Blah, Blah, snore, snore.

You may be having those feelings too and I want to let you know that it's NORMAL.

These feelings come from a place of lack (or referred to as a 'lack mindset'). Worrying that you're not going to have enough, do enough or be enough.

I have a question, on that point. Who decided what was deemed enough? Who made the rules and where is he? I'd like to meet him. So I can punch him in the f***ing face.

Who is this person that we feel we must stand up to? That there is some scale or measurement that we're supposed to meet and if we don't, well we've basically failed and our life will be shit.

It's a bit like the fairground rides I could never go on as a kid because I was always too short. I'd stand next to the wooden cut out of the deranged looking child eating candy floss but the top of my head never quite made it to the line no matter how much I stretched my neck or tried to stand on tip toes without the ride operator noticing....

So every time my friends would clamber onto the rides and spin and whiz and whirl and scream with excitement, I'd stand at the bottom holding bags and purses trying not to cry and wanting the world to swallow me up. And what did I decide in that moment? Yep, you guessed it. That I wasn't enough. I wasn't tall enough (which ultimately I decided to mean I wasn't good enough) because they'd missed me when handing out the tall genes on that day…

Anyway, back to letting go.

Jim Rohn said it best when he said 'You become the average of the five people you spend the most time with' and he couldn't be more spot on.

What does it mean?

Think about the five people you spend the most time with for a moment. This may be your circle of friends, it may be work colleagues, family. It might even be online friendships and relationships you have formed as a result of your Business and Social Media.

Do these people spend a considerable amount of time complaining? Moaning? Always seeming to struggle? Do they support you and your business? Would you say they're overly negative? Do you find yourself gossiping when you're with them? Bitching about other people, complaining about how broke you are or moaning that you hate your job?

Remember that what you focus on you attract. So when you're with these people (or communicating with them online) you'll be attracting back similar attitudes, levels of success, characteristics and personalities. If these are the types of conversations you're having (i.e. 'focusing on') then this is what you'll be attracting more of. You'll be attracting more of these kinds of people or more events and situations to MAKE you complain, moan, bitch and gossip and feel crap about things.

If however you spend your time with people who light you up, who celebrate your wins and motivate you when you're feeling stuck, who inspire you, who have a positive, grateful, abundant outlook on life and who are attracting success for themselves....what do you think you'll attract into YOUR life?

That's right. More people like that and more things in your life to feel grateful and abundant for. More wins, more successes, more money - Yes Please!

It's so easy to get drawn into the drudginess (I may have totally just made up a word there but I'm going with it...) of everyday life that we don't take the time to stop and look around us at who we're allowing into our circle. We meet people at a certain juncture in our life but then allow them to come along for the ride, even perhaps long after our destinations have changed.

I used to feel guilty about wanting to avoid certain friends because they were so negative all the time. Or stressing at certain gatherings because I felt I had to put on a show with some people to fit in. That who I was wasn't good enough and that I needed to be better, smarter, thinner, funnier, prettier. The list goes on and on. I was so desperate to fit in (thanks to the school bullies who you'll hear more about in a minute) that

I would go along with what everyone else wanted to do all the time. I would mirror what they said and did, how they acted, out of fear of - heaven forbid - having my own opinion on something.

I'd find myself complaining about my boyfriend, bitching about work colleagues and generally being drawn into conversations that just made me squirmy and uncomfortable on the inside, scared shitless that if I didn't I'd be picked on again. I'd be called weird, I'd be the outsider, I'd be left friendless and alone.

When my friend shared with me her thoughts on my positive postings I did let it get to me for a while. I went back to worrying yet again about what people thought of me, feeling anxious every time I put something on social media in case I offended someone or annoyed them or made them roll their eyes. I hated the idea of people thinking badly of me so much, that for a short while I went back to posting about how crap my job was, how much I hated my boss, how of course it was raining on my way to work and I'd forgotten my umbrella as that's just 'typical' and the way my life goes...

But something didn't feel right. Something had shifted. I had absolutely no idea what it was at the time but all I could put it down to was a weird feeling inside (I'll be sharing more of this in Chapter 5 when we'll be discussing trusting your instincts but don't skip ahead as there's more you need to know here before you can get there.)

What I came to understand, and what I'm now sharing with you in this book, was totally and completely enlightening. Illuminating even. In fact I'd go so far as saying it was freeing.

I'm now very conscious of who I allow into my circle and I've accepted that some people will come and go. Some people are only meant to come into our lives for a short amount of time (a year or two as opposed to a decade I mean) and some will have such an impact that you know they're there for the long haul.

I still care about that 'exhausted' friend of course but I'm nowhere near as attached to her as I once was. I no longer hold on to the desperation of wanting to be loved, NEEDING to feel good enough that I would filter and hide and hold back certain aspects of me that I now know fully make me - ME.

And once I let go of the need to hold on to relationships like the one with the exhausted friend and others, my success soared. My confidence soared, my belief soared and my income soared. I'd spent 10 years 'trying' to build a business, the whole time worrying about what people thought. Not wanting to talk about my many business ventures (there were several!) if my circle at that time brought it up. Feeling awkward, embarrassed, ashamed and really quite small. I felt like they were belittling it so much at the time, that I wanted to wait until I had loads of success before being really open about it.

Once I let go and changed my thinking towards the people I surrounded myself with, I generated half a million in sales in two years.

Now, don't get me wrong, I'm not saying this is the ONLY reason for my new found success, it was a combination of everything I share in this book, together with lots of trial and error in terms of marketing and the skill side of running a business...but it was, without a shadow of a doubt, fundamental.

Once I spent less time worrying about what other people were thinking about me, I had SO MUCH more time to focus on myself. What I thought about myself, how I talked to and about myself, I had more time to work on self-development and my mindset. And then when I did start to see more success, I had the confidence - and the perfect circle of people - to feel good enough to share it. To celebrate it. To OWN it. This then allows more success to come pouring in.

Remember that people will come and go from your life. Everyone we meet and build relationships with we do so for a reason. You're attracting these people into your life. The Universe gives you what and who you need at the time - but it's up to you to be aware of perhaps when that need is no longer there.

A couple of decades ago there was someone in my life who was the most important person on the planet to me. For privacy reasons we'll call her *Amy*. *Amy* had come into my life EXACTLY when I needed her. I'd

35

spent three whole years of my life at Secondary School feeling miserable, desperate and terribly alone. I'd started at that Secondary School at the age of 11 with a wonderful best friend who was going to be my BFF forever and ever and ever.

Forever and ever and ever turned out to actually only be that first week of Secondary School until she was taken under the wing of the class bitches (aka the 'cool' popular girls) and my BFF decided she no longer wanted to even be an F let alone a BFF and I was left very alone that Monday morning in a new school with no friends.

Then the taunting started. Then the physical abuse. Then, worse, the emotional abuse. I felt so lost with who I was and who I was meant to be in order to be accepted that I'd spend my time in class in a foggy haze and eating my lunch by myself behind a wall in the Playground.

I was so desperate to find someone who understood me, who allowed me to be me and accepted me for it. Finally, in my 4th year the Universe responded (I'm still two decades away from understanding it was the Universe at this point and just thought it was coincidence but I was so over the moon that I didn't care or question it!).

The 4th year was the year that we chose our elective subjects for our GCSE exams and we were put into sets for our non-electives such as Math, Science and English. Now thankfully because the bitches, sorry I mean popular girls, had spent so much time and attention on making fun of me that their grades weren't up to scratch and I hadn't let mine slip enough in an attempt to fit in meant that we chose different subjects for our Exams or were put into different sets. So we had no classes together. At all.

I was now in new classes with lots of other kids also in new classes and I felt like this was a complete fresh start. I could walk into my classes without feeling anxious that I'd be tripped up or have something thrown at me. Nobody in this half of the year really even knew who I was and so I could just be me.

And on my very first day in that 4th year I met *Amy*. I sat down at an empty desk in English Class feeling a little nervous but relieved I didn't have to pretend to be anyone else when in she came. She looked around the room, saw an empty space next to me and asked if she could sit there. That was all it took. Pretty much instantly she became my best friend. My Soul Sister. We'd hang out every day after school, pass notes to each other in class and from that point on we became a 'pair'. Boyfriends knew they had to deal with it, other kids would ask where the other was if only one of us was there. She was my world. My rock. And the exact person I needed.

This friendship was formed at the age of 15 and lasted a good 15 years more. As we grew older and our lives were taking turns in different directions I knew deep down that we were drifting apart but I wouldn't let myself think it. I was so resistant to it. *Amy* had been such an enormous part of my life that how was it even possible that we wouldn't be soul mates our entire lives? That's just crazy! And so I resisted it. I forced it. I think she forced it too though I've never actually asked her.

Once I found the world of the Law of Attraction and having a positive mindset and started seeing success in my business it was almost like we didn't have anything in common anymore. We'd make small talk but it would start to feel awkward and uncomfortable and like we were going through the motions. Meeting up every few months for a catch up because we felt we should, not because we had a huge desire to.

I remember feeling incredibly sad when this realisation first hit me. It felt like the end of an era. A heartbreak or a bereavement even. But I now fully understand that *Amy* came to me when I needed her. She helped shape so much of my life, affected who I am today and has given me so many wonderful memories that still make me laugh out loud today. And don't get me wrong, it's not like we've officially announced the end of our friendship or anything. If I see her in the street (which hasn't actually happened yet) then of course I'll stop and chat. And if ever she needed me for something I'd be there in a heartbeat. It's just my world is very different to her world now. Not better, just different. And I need people in my circle who will encourage and inspire and motivate. Who understand what I'm doing or at least why I'm doing it. Who are striving for success in their life and business and who won't settle for ordinary.

But just in the off chance you're reading this *Amy* (you'll know who you are), Thank you. From the bottom of my heart. Thank you.

In contrast, I have another friend, who is by far my most favourite person on the planet after my daughter (Ok, and my husband - I have to say that in case he reads this...love you Gareth ;)). He came into my life at around the same time as *Amy* but our friendship didn't really blossom for a few years. It then grew and grew and we became closer and closer and I've had the privilege of calling him my friend for over 20 years (at the time of writing). The word friend doesn't even feel like it does it justice to be fair. He's the "Guidefather" to my daughter (like a Godfather but without the religious stuff) and I trust him with my life. I can be 100% completely and totally me. No filtering, no hiding. Just me. He accepts me as I am and the feeling is mutual. He supports my business, he respects my goals and he encourages me to keep moving forward. I know he will continue to be an important part of my life for very many years to come.

So letting go simply means being mindful of who you surround yourself with. If the relationships are no longer serving you, if you feel they're holding you back from being the person you know deep down you can be, if you feel you're going in different directions, striving for different things and have very different goals and aspirations for your life then it may be time to have an 'audit'. You may feel sad at the time but remember that everything happens for a reason and everything in it's own time.

You have to ask yourself how much do you want it? Do you want to get to age 75 and wonder what your life could have been like? Do you want to feel resentment, lack or loss or that you missed so many opportunities because you were so afraid to let people go?

Or do you want to feel abundance and joy and a heart full of gratitude as you look back on your life and ALL the amazing people that came in and out, some staying for longer than others but every single one adding to it in some way and all the success and experiences you enjoyed as a result?

I know which I want.

And if you're reading this book then I'm sure you know which one you want too.

So what now? Well this isn't the part of the book where I tell you to divorce your spouse if he or she is a moody arsehole at times or to leave everyone you know behind and start a new life on Mars…

But I do encourage you to really start to think about your 'circle' and who is currently in it.

Make a list of all the characteristics and traits and personalities that you would love to see in your 'ideal circle'. What do these people spend their time doing? How do they act? What do they say? How do they react when you talk about your business? Or success? Or money? What goals do they have? Are they negative or positive? Do they focus on what they have or what they don't have? How do you feel when you're around them?

Really spend some time on this. Give yourself some distraction free time to really think about this. Write it in a pretty journal, scribble it on a bit of paper, put it into the notes section of your phone - whatever works for you. Just make the time to do this task.

Keep writing until you can't think of anything else. Then leave it for 24 hours and come back to it. See if there are final things that have come up for you that you want to add.

Once you have your complete list (it's very likely you'll continue adding to it over the next few days so don't worry) then look through it and compare what you've written to the people who are currently in your life. Do they fit this 'profile'? Who does and who doesn't? Again, this isn't about cutting every single person out of your life, it's about being aware and mindful in order that you know what needs to change, if anything.

There are no big announcements that need to be made. No fireworks or fanfare. There is certainly no need to call up your friends and family one by one and tell them that you're no longer putting up with their bullshit and you're cutting them out of your life to make way for new awesome people...

But if there are people in your circle who are a negative influence in your life then make the conscious effort to spend less and less time with them. Choosing instead to spend time with those in your circle who are a positive influence and on the lookout for new potential candidates! If it's time to let them go then you'll notice one day that it's been three months since you've spoken and you're ok with that.

So how do you know if someone is a negative influence on your life?

Here are a few sure signs that you may need to 'let go' of a relationship:

You don't 100% enjoy the prospect of a 'catch up' with them because all they do is moan all the time.

They draw you into their negative discussions, bitching and gossip.

You feel drained, tired or low energy after you've spent time with them (whether in person or online.)

You find yourself making small talk because you don't have anything in common anymore.

You find yourself agreeing with them just to make them happy even though it's the opposite of what you actually believe.

They make you feel crap, ashamed, embarrassed, small or any other shitty feeling when you talk about your business, success, money or your goals.

You feel you have to hide parts of yourself from them and you're regularly filtering what you say.

You actually dread going to a social function when you know they'll be there (you'd think that would be a big indicator but it's amazing how many people - myself included - just go along with it, a little oblivious, for the sake of an 'easy life').

If you have people in your life now that fall under those statements above then there's a good chance that you're not as successful as you want to be or could be. Because you're spending your time with people who bring you down, keep your energy low and force you to focus on the negative. None of which are conducive to manifesting your dream life.

I know that may seem blunt but I want you to REALLY understand the importance of this message.

So make your list of the people you want in your life and then start taking the steps to attract those people to you.

And if you feel like you need a little more guidance, keep reading for the Chapter on Trusting Your Instincts!

Chapter 5

TRUST YOUR INSTINCTS

This chapter goes kind of hand in hand with the last chapter about letting go of negative influences in your life and is probably going to be one of my favourite chapters. I know this before I've even written it, because of the impact it's had on my life and the impact it can have on yours too.

As I'm sat writing this chapter in the Premier Cabin of my BA flight back home to the UK from the States, where I've just had the most incredible week, earning multiple five figures speaking and coaching at an Info Marketing Retreat, I still have to pinch myself a little that this is my life now and how very different it could have been.

Let me take you back to February 2016....

I remember the excitement that was literally whizzing through my body, causing my fingers to tingle and a smile that I could NOT wipe off my face. I couldn't sit still, I was literally BUZZING!

After spending sooooo many years feeling a bit lost, knowing that there was something out there that I was MEANT to be doing. That there was a way I could earn money AND do something I love, that I didn't just have to 'go to work just to pay the bills' but that I could really do something amazing and impact so many others in the process. After spending 10 years trying to build a business in Network Marketing and Direct Sales and really really struggling to 'find my place', I finally felt like I had found what I'd been looking for. What had been missing for so long.

I was fascinated, excited, curious, terrified and exhilarated all at the same time. I had stumbled upon the area of Mindset, Law of Attraction and Neuroplasticity (Brain Rewiring stuff) and it had absolutely blown me away.

I KNEW this was what I should be doing. I didn't quite know HOW I was going to do it at this point but that didn't matter. It had lit a fire inside my soul and I was so excited for what was to come. I had enrolled in a Happiness Life Coaching Course and a Law of Attraction Practitioner Course and I was so bloody excited!!

Then I told my upline in my Network Marketing company. Someone who I truly believed was a friend, someone I could turn to for support and encouragement. I'd known her a couple of years and had followed her when she moved from one MLM company to another, because I thought she had my back…

I told her that I had found this new interest, it was amazing, I was fascinated by it, I knew I had to look into it more and see where it took me.

And this is what she said.

'Well I'll be honest, you're never going to make any money from that. You'll never turn that into a business and get anything from it. I'm changing lives! But if you want a new hobby then go for it.'

Yep. Word for word that's what she said. It's been almost three years (at the time of writing) but I remember it as if it were yesterday. I remember it because it floored me. I was so shocked that this person who I truly thought was my friend could be so unsupportive. I mean, even if you think those things you don't say them right?!

I remember because it made me feel so crap. That I could go from literally buzzing to my heart sinking into my feet in a split second. Maybe she was right? Maybe it was a waste of time, a pipedream, who would ever take me seriously as a coach anyway right? I couldn't make Network Marketing work so why should I think I'd be better at anything else?

But I also remember it because it's the first time I REALLY listened to my gut. My instincts were telling me I was MEANT to do this. That whatever business I could build, whatever income I could make, whatever impact I could have on the world - THIS is what I was called to do. My 'purpose' if you like.

So I did something I had never really done before. I listened to my gut.

I decided there and then that I would no longer let anyone else define my worth, tell me what I should be doing, where I should be spending my time, how much I could earn or how I should live my life. I felt this new power inside of me and this just burned even stronger when within 30 minutes of the call, I had been removed from the Team Chats on Facebook and deleted as a friend...

I could have let her words stop me. To define me. Allow the doubt and fear to take over.

But in the moment, I chose MY future. I made the decision.

It was EMPOWERING!

Now here I am just three years later, a full time Law of Attraction and Success Mindset Practitioner, Trainer, Speaker, Coach and Author. Free from the boss, the commute, the capped pay, the time spent away from my daughter, the stress, the anxiety, the desperation. Earning more than I have ever done before and doing something that literally lights me up. That fills my heart AND my bank account with absolute joy. Writing my second book while on a plane from Reno where I hit a huge milestone in my business - generating over half a million dollars in sales in the last 20 months.

I've been flown half way around the world for an all-expenses paid trip to coach some amazing people and help them make a life changing decision to step into the best version of themselves. I've met some truly inspiring, motivating people. People that I've looked up to for the last three years and now I'm sharing the stage with them and dancing with them at the VIP After Parties. I've stepped fully out of my comfort zone but that's where the magic happens right?

As you're reading this book then I can tell you for sure that you can have this too! You can literally be, do and have whatever you want. Your only limitations are the ones you put on yourself.

There will always be people who don't support you. Who put you down, who make you feel like shit, who take your power away by telling you what you can and can't do. Don't let them. Don't let them define who you are and what your potential is.

48

If there is something stirring inside of you, if there is an idea you've been thinking about but you wonder if it's stupid, if your instincts are telling you to follow a certain path, talk to a particular person, do a certain something, or NOT do something then follow that instinct.

Listen to your gut.

I did three years ago and I've continued to do so on a number of occasions since and every time I have, it has absolutely paid off. It's part of the manifesting process, to 'trust' that everything will work out for the best for you. That if you listen to your intuition and act on it (the Universe bloody loves inspired action!) then you're opening the path for abundance.

So don't let anyone else steal your power. Listen to your instincts, your intuition, your inspiration.

So how exactly do you listen to your inspiration? Trust your instincts or follow your gut?

It starts with being more mindful when thinking about your business, your goals, your life. Be more aware of the thoughts that go on inside your head, notice how your body feels when you have these thoughts, what is that 7 year old part of you convincing you to do or not do?

We can convince ourselves we're not good enough and therefore shouldn't do something within a few seconds. That's all it takes for us to ignore what we REALLY want and stay where it's comfortable instead.

Let me give you an example of how that might go:

You: 'Oh wow, the chance to speak on stage at the next company event, I'd totally love to do that, I think I really want to start speaking on stage more and that could be the perfect stepping stone!'

Your body: Feels tingly with excitement, maybe butterflies in your tummy and a smile (even slight) on your face.

Your thoughts: It won't be easy though as there will be lots of competition. Do you remember when you were 12 and you had to speak at the front of the class and you couldn't remember your words and a squeak came out and everyone laughed? You don't want that again do you?

Your body: Brain is sending stress chemicals around your body, the butterflies have turned to a sick feeling and maybe your palms start to sweat.

You: 'I'm not sure I'd win that so I won't bother. I don't really have the time anyway'.

I bet if you can think back to things you have wanted to be, do or have you've talked yourself out of it on many occasion. Listening to that voice in your head that tells you you're not good enough, that reminds you of that time when you were nine and you failed at something as it wants to keep you safe. That's its only job remember.

I had all sorts of thoughts going around my head three years ago when I was signing up for that Happiness Life Coaching Course and then told my upline about it. Wondering if it was just a bit of a whim, something else I was going to try and build a business from and fail (as everything else had failed over the previous 10 years), terrified about what people would think of me, would they think I was weird and 'tree huggy' if I started to go a bit 'woo woo'.

But I also had something else going on too. My instincts were fighting it. Something inside (and I'm not sure I can even explain what it was which I know isn't overly insightful in terms of helping you to understand it but I think you just know when you know). This time felt different. I still had the butterflies in my stomach and the excitement whizzing around my body despite everything telling me I shouldn't do it. I was still trying to reason with myself for why I SHOULD do it even though I had no idea what was going to happen. And it just felt right.

So really start to be more aware, listen to your body, listen to your initial thoughts and words in the first two seconds after thinking about a goal or something you want to achieve. Then grab a journal or a notebook or a scrap piece of paper it doesn't really matter and note down how your body feels when you're excited about something. As it will be different for everyone. My body will show its excitement in a slight variation to

51

how yours might so note down what happens to your body when you're excited (even if nervous with it). When you think about your goals, your dream life, the success you want to create. Do you feel a tingling in your fingers or toes? Do you feel a throbbing in your head? Do you feel shivers down your spine? Butterflies in your stomach? Note down how it feels for you to be in this state and then be more aware when your body sends you these signals.

Now if you're anything like I used to be and suffer with 'shiny object syndrome' (which is actually just a lack of clarity by the way) then you may be wondering how you can tell whether something is an 'instinct' or just another shiny object to steer you off track. It all goes back to your thoughts and emotions the second you think about it (even if you keep coming back to it over and over again). How do you feel and think about it BEFORE you start convincing yourself not to do it? Do you feel excited? Intrigued? Buzzing? Also consider whether it is something that you ACTUALLY want. Ask yourself whether it is something that you actually want to achieve/be/do/have or whether it's something that you feel you 'should' have, that you see others having and so assume should want the same, that other seemingly successful people have it so you tell yourself you ought to as well. Or is it something that actually gets you giddy with excitement, that makes you smile, that lights you up? This will be a sure indicator of whether it's something worth pursuing.

If you're still really not sure, note down the idea in the back of a notepad and come back to it a few times over the coming weeks. Does how you feel around it change? Does the excitement wear off? Just ensure you're not taking so long to decide about something that you talk yourself out of it.

There's also a good chance that you're concerned that if you do listen to your instincts and it doesn't pan out that you've wasted even more time. Right?

The honest truth is that you won't really know. Until you do it. Some instincts will be awesome decisions, some not so much. But EVERYTHING happens for a reason and everything is a lesson or a part of our journey in some way. So ask yourself, would you rather go after what you want and you discover it wasn't actually what you want but along the way you found something else even more amazing....or would you rather not try and stay in your 'comfortable' place, always wondering what could have been?

I know which I would choose.

And I'm trusting that you're now choosing your instincts too.

Go after what you want with excitement, courage and determination. It's already yours for the taking - go get it!

Chapter 6

JUST DO THE DAMN THING!

This Chapter wasn't actually in the first draft of this book. I'd sent it off to my awesome publishing consultant and editor, was feeling all smug and proud of myself because I'd finished my book….and then while driving to my friend's one evening, trying to weigh up the pros and cons of a particular business decision that I'd been thinking about all week and spending far too much time over it yet again, I was hit with inspiration. And it was then that I knew this chapter had to be included. And that's why I've put it right here, after the Chapter on Trusting Your Instincts.

Because I want you to understand that this crappy belief about not being 'good enough' can show up for you in a variety of ways. It's not always the more obvious 'what will they think of me?', 'he left me because I'm not pretty enough', and 'I wish I was as thin as her' kind of conversations that we have with ourselves. It can show up in the actions we take (or more often than not DON'T take) and this is never more apparent than when dealing with our businesses.

During the 'Starting Out Phase' of my entrepreneurial journey (which lasted 10 years FYI) I spent so much time worrying about every single decision. Whether I was making the 'right' decision, the 'best' decision.

Which Social Media Platform should I use?

Which Network Marketing Company should I join?

Which Website hosting company should I use?

What should my domain name be?

What should my cover photo on my social media be like?

I spent so much time worrying about making the wrong decision that it took me forever to make ANY decision.

I must have wasted YEARS staring at Website Platforms, researching every detail of my decisions on the Internet, asking a gazillion other people what they thought and what they use and what worked for them, tweaking logos - which ultimately I never used because I'd spent so long creating them that by the time I was happy with them, I'd changed my branding, or my business name or the direction I wanted to take my business in because - guess what, Shiny Object Syndrome had hit again and I was questioning whether what I was doing was 'good enough' and instead thought I'd jump on the next craze, the next 'big thing' because that's what I saw other 'successful people' doing.

I do wonder how much further along in my business I could have been. How much money I could have made, how much impact I could have had on the world. I fully believe that everything happens for a reason and everything in its own time but I really REALLY wish for you that you don't go down the same path. I don't want you to spend years worrying that you're not making the right decision, worrying that you're not good enough, worrying that you're not making the perfect decision so that you're not doing ANYTHING and instead I want to encourage you to just do the damn thing already!

Because, really, what's going to happen if you choose to go with one email provider company and 60 days down the line you decide that actually it doesn't have the features you like so you decide to cancel that membership and go with a different one? Well, sure, you spent a little bit of time on it and maybe you've spent about £30 but at least you made a decision. And now you've been able to break down your options because you know that's not the one that you want to go for and you want to go for a different one instead. So really is it the end of the world if you choose one and decide that actually it's not a perfect fit for you?

Is it the end of the world if you decide to go down one business route but then shift gears and change direction a while down the road?

Gone are the days and the times where being an entrepreneur means you're a car salesman or that you have to spend thousands on a franchise or on buying a commercial property. In this day and age with social media, with online marketing and with online businesses taking the world by storm, with women really finding their place and building strong successful businesses that are leaving legacies for generations, it's so much easier to build these businesses. So you don't have to fit into one box, you don't have to just pick one thing and do that. If something doesn't work out, pick yourself up and choose something else and that's okay because at least you did SOMETHING!

It's very very rare that it will actually be a life or death scenario when considering your options in relation to your business and yet so many people (myself included) waste so much time out of absolute fear that we'll make the wrong decision, instead of just having the belief and confidence to move forward, knowing that it's absolutely possible to make a course correct down the road if necessary.

This fear causes so much chaos and confusion in our minds that it completely halts our growth and progress.

And where does this fear come from?

The belief that we're not good enough.

'What if I make the wrong decision and people find out about it?'
'What If I make the wrong decision and it costs me a lot of money/time/effort - what will my family say?'

'What if I make the wrong decision and someone else makes a better one? They'll be more successful than me.'

'What if I make the wrong decision and people know that I'm not an expert?'

What if. What if. What if.

Did you know that the 'What If' question is the most common question we ask ourselves?

But it's what you put after it that determines your success.

Usually it will be followed by a negative as above (What if I fail? What if I lose all my money?).

But imagine if you followed it with a positive instead...

'What if I make the right decision and it propels me into success?!'
'What if I make this decision and I make SO MUCH MONEY?!'
'What if I make the right decision and I reach my goals faster?!'

Doesn't that feel better? Doesn't that make you want to smile when reading it/saying it instead?

Just to be clear though - there are no 'right or wrong' decisions. The only 'wrong' decision is the one you didn't take.

Remember, trust your instincts. If deep down you know you want to do something, pick something, choose a particular option - then DO it! Because - depending on what the decision in question is of course - it's unlikely it will cause that much distress, heartache, financial ruin or stoning from the local community if a little down the line you choose to make a different decision instead.

But NOT making any decision? Well that can cause weeks, months or even years of overwhelm, stress and lack of momentum in your business and life. How much money are you actually LOSING by not making the decision? How much time are you throwing away?

So I encourage you to start making confident decisions in your business (and in life of course - it's all connected).

Because that's where growth happens.

That's where clarity is formed, self-confidence is built and where new beliefs are programmed to extend the walls of your comfort zone.

That's ultimately where abundance comes pouring in.

So here's what I want you to do...

Next time you have a decision that you're pondering. Maybe you're stuck between 2 or 3 (or more) options and you just can't decide which one to go with.

Grab a piece of paper and write down as many of the 'What If' negative questions and statements that come to mind when thinking about that decision.

When you have nothing else to add (stop when you feel like you're forcing it) then grab a fresh sheet of paper and write down a 'What If' positive for every negative that you've written. Literally flip it on its head from a negative question to a positive one.

So for example:

'What if I choose Option A and it's the wrong one?' becomes 'What if I choose Option A and it's the BEST decision?!'

'What if I do this and I don't make any sales?' would become 'What if I do this and I have SO MANY SALES coming in?!'

Then when you have your positive list, put it up on your wall or on your desk, somewhere that you'll see it clearly and write out the options that you're considering on a piece of paper and put it next to it. Look at the options, look at your 'What If' positive list and then PICK ONE! Listen to your gut, go with your first instincts, Circle it, underline it, scribble out the other one, whatever's going to work for you —

And then get to work!

Do The Damn Thing!

<u>Chapter 7</u>

JUST DO YOU

'Today you are you, that is truer than true, there is no one alive more youer than you' ~ *Dr Seuss*

Ok, can we talk about the 'fake it till you make it' stuff for a second?

Because I feel like this needs to be said.

When it comes to your mindset, faking it until you make it can be very sound advice. Your brain doesn't know the difference between what is ACTUALLY right or wrong, true or false. It literally acts on what you tell it. So using positive affirmations telling yourself that you're confident, that you're rolling in the money and making a powerful impact on the world is a great tool at your disposal (more of that in a later chapter).

62

However, having spent 10 years in the Network Marketing industry before building the business I have now, I came across the 'fake it until you make it' marketing concept on so many occasions. It left me feeling sleazy, dirty and just plain dishonest. So I didn't partake in it. And yeah, maybe that's why I wasn't successful at it, but at least I kept my morals...

I was involved in one particular team with this one particular Upline who crossed the line so many times with the 'FITYMI' concept that I don't think she could even see the line anymore.

Here are just some of the things she did in order to 'appear' successful in her business to 'encourage' (con) people into buying her products and joining her team:

She would walk into a luxury shoe shop, try on a pair of designer and/or expensive shoes, take a photo of herself in said shoes and post it all over social media exclaiming things like 'Look what I just bought with my commissions this month!' or 'I'm living the high life thanks to my [Company XXX] commission!' and would then put the shoes back and walk out. No shame.

She had lip filler surgery and then posted before and after photos, again all over social media, claiming that it was the company's collagen boosting lip gloss that had given her such amazing results.

She would pull up next to an expensive car parked by the side of the road or in a car park, stand next to it, shoot a photo of herself next to said stranger's car (again no shame) and excitedly announce to the world of social media that she was so blessed to have hit the car promotion that month.

She encouraged us to do the same 'fake it till you make it' things like purchase a load of stock ourselves, put them into individual bags and post about all the orders we had received that week...

Basically we were encouraged to lie about the things we had been able to achieve in order to convince people to join our teams and buy our stuff.

This is just plain wrong. People are going to invest in you and your business because they resonate with YOU. Because they hear your story and they GET your story. Because you're honest and open and genuine and you can show them how you got from point A to point B and how you can help them get there too.

Not because you're standing your fake ass next to a Ferrari pretending you own it...

#JustSayin

All the 'fake it till you make it' rubbish does is make us feel a little bit uncomfortable, a bit dishonest, not in alignment with what we're doing (so we won't be successful at it) and just leaves us with this overwhelming feeling of not being good enough.

If we were good enough we wouldn't have to pretend we were buying awesome shit because we actually would be buying awesome shit, right?

This causes us to feel shame, fear, doubt, overwhelm, panic and all the other guests you DO NOT want to party with if you're looking to have a good time.

So why do we feel the need to bend the truth on social media? (and it doesn't just stop there). Pretending to the world that we're 'successful' according to somebody's idea of what that means, yet the whole time feeling stressed and confused?

It goes back to that 7 year old version of you that decided you're not 'good' enough. That you need to be someone better, more successful, different to how you are. When, in fact, who you are right now is absolutely perfect. You're exactly where you're meant to be and that's ok. It's when we fight it, deny it, spend all our time worrying about being someone else that we get off track, lose the path and go round in circles (we'll probably eventually get back on the path but after wasting a whole lot of time).

Social media has A LOT to answer for in respect to so much of the stressing and worrying that goes on in our heads. Because we only see a tiny glimpse of what people want to show us AND we see what we want to see. We make up stories in our head without even realising it about why someone else has it easier, why they're luckier, why they're better than you because they have A, B and C even though if you stopped to think about it you would realise you don't even want A, B and C so there's no point stressing about it!

So please stop comparing yourself to others. You have no idea what crappy limiting beliefs their 7 year old version of themselves is throwing their way, you don't know how much they've struggled, how long it took to get them there and their version of success may look a whole lot different to yours.

That woman on stage receiving an award in her company? She may have bought her way there. Or she may have been 'trying' for 20 years. That Upline who has joined a company and brought in 100 new team members in her first 2 weeks? She may have pulled everyone over from a team within a previous company.

Don't compare YOUR journey to someone else's as it's not the same journey. You may be on the same path for a tiny part of the route but there are always crossroads, turnings and forks in the road that lead to different destinations. So instead of stressing about whether you're as successful as your companion on the path at that particular time, enjoy the journey instead. Stop to smell the roses, chat with your fellow path takers and keep looking ahead at YOUR OWN path.

So next time you find yourself scrolling through social media comparing yourself to others, worrying that you're not good enough here's what I want you to do:

Are you ready?

Turn off Social Media.

Yep. It's as easy as that (and actually, one of the hardest things to do in this day and age!). If you find yourself falling into comparitis mode shut down your tabs on your computer, close the apps on your phone, take a deep breath and say to yourself 'I am exactly who I am meant to be and I am successful exactly as I am'.

Then go do something fun.

Put on some music and dance around your room like a loon, go for a run if that's your idea of fun (it's not mine but you know, each to their own!). Put on a funny movie, call up a friend. Whatever it is that makes you feel good and takes your mind out of where it was. Interrupt the negative thought processes that were going on and switch things up.

Here are a few further words of encouragement to some things you may be feeling right now:

Worried that if you just be you people won't like it? Then they're not your people. They're not the ones who will buy your products, take out your service, book your programs or join your team. The ones who resonate with you and your story will be the Tribe that grows to know, like, trust and love you. Who stick with you whatever vulnerabilities you show to them.

Worried that people will think you're ridiculous? Then they're not your people - see above.

Worried that they won't find you interesting enough? Then they're not your people - see above.

Worried that they won't think you're 'good' enough? Then they're not your people - see above.

You get the idea right? Your success will come when YOU decide that you're good enough. When you stop trying to be someone else and show up as the best version of you that you can be each and every day. Even if that means going live on social media in your pyjamas while eating a donut. If that's you being YOU at your youest, then own it. Honour it. Thank the Universe for it.

And don't you dare ever, EVER apologise for it.

Chapter 8

GRATITUDE ATTITUDE

'When you are grateful fear disappears and abundance appears' - *Tony Robbins.*

'The more thankful I became the more my bounty increased' - *Oprah Winfrey*

So this is the part of the book where we talk about Gratitude. I know, I know 'insert eye roll here'. It seems like every person under the sun teaching about transformation talks about the importance of Gratitude - so much so that it feels like an over used, worn out cliché.

But there's a reason it's talked about so much.

Because it works.

Plain and simple.

Fact.

If you ask any successful, confident person out there what their secret is, I guarantee they'll talk about Gratitude. Sure, there are other elements to a person's success and to getting the Law of Attraction working for you but Gratitude is the foundation of EVERYTHING.

It comes down to this - if you're not grateful for what you have, you won't get anything better.

If you want to start feeling more confident in the near future then you need to start feeling grateful NOW.

So many times have I heard (and I used to say this myself so I'm no stranger to it):

I'll feel really grateful when I'm successful.
When I've made more money I'll feel really grateful.
I don't have anything to be grateful for, I'm broke and in a dead end job and my business is just an expensive hobby! I'll feel grateful when I have more to be grateful for.

Unfortunately, if you find yourself saying this or thinking this, then I hate to break it to you but you'll never be successful. You'll never feel more confident and your income won't increase.

It's just the way it works.

Remember that what you focus on you attract. This could not be truer than when dealing with gratitude. Think about it for a moment - if you're constantly complaining about how broke you are, how annoying your partner is, how much you hate your job, how it sucks that it's Monday again....bla bla bla..... What do you think you'll attract to you?

That's right. More stuff to feel bad about, more people that piss you off, more traffic jams on the way to work. It works with your emotions, habits and beliefs too. You'll be attracting more doubt, more fear, more anxiety. More things to worry about. More distractions and procrastinations.

On the other hand, what do you think you'll attract to you when you regularly talk about your wins? When you express all the things you're grateful for, when you approach tasks with positivity and are thankful for all the opportunities that come your way?

Spot on. You'll attract MORE things to be grateful for, more people that lift you up, more experiences and situations that push you out of your comfort zone and fill you up with confidence.

71

There have been a number of techniques that have helped me achieve the success I've created today, and I share most of them within this book, but the biggest for me has to be expressing more gratitude and joy every single day.

Because it wasn't always the case I assure you!

I had a very clear reminder of this recently. You know on Facebook there's the 'Memories' function where it shows you everything you posted on that day since joining Facebook? Well my posts from before 2016 are just downright depressing! Sure there are the occasional celebratory ones but most of them are complaining about something pretty unimportant.

One particular reminder that came up recently from a post I made in about 2009, simply said 'Monday. Great. Raining. Great'. Yep, that was what I decided to share with the World (or at least the friends I had on Facebook) on that raining Monday in 2009. Out of everything in my life, that was what I decided to focus on.

Now, I don't actually remember that day and I'm sure nothing particularly traumatic or newsworthy happened but I'm also fairly certain that I would have had a pretty miserable day. The day at work probably dragged its arse, my boss was most likely in a mood, I probably stepped in a puddle and had to walk around with a wet sock all day and so on and so on.

Because that's how our brains work. I just didn't know it at the time.

So I stress again the importance of gratitude.

I know it can seem a little weird to come to terms with and I've been asked a number of times whether declaring that you're content with what you have now means you don't want anything more and so won't achieve any of your goals but just trust me when I say it doesn't work like that.

This isn't about not wanting anything more and not declaring your goals or setting intentions and taking the steps to create your Dream Life, this is about focusing on what you do already have, staying in a positive, grateful, abundant, joyous frame of mind as often as possible. This is then the perfect state to be in to attract more abundance to you.

So here's the pretty cool thing with Gratitude...... there is ALWAYS something to be grateful for. I promise you. You may be wondering how you find things to be grateful for when you're in debt, exhausted, stressed but I assure you, if you look for them, you'll find them.

They don't need to be huge earth shattering, life changing things, like 10k months or a five bedroom home by the Ocean to have an effect. Your brain and the Universe does not discriminate, it does not hand out

Abundance Awards to those who have the biggest accomplishments or have the fanciest homes or the sexiest cars.

It is about the frequency of the gratitude and the emotion you apply to it, not the actual thing you're grateful for. The only difference between whether the concept works or not is how you FEEL about it and how often you do it.

For example, writing three things in a pretty butterfly journal in June but then not touching it again or expressing gratitude again until December isn't going to do very much so don't expect miracles in that department.

But when you can start to express gratitude DAILY, that's when you'll see things changing and you'll feel the shift One day you'll just notice that you feel happier, that things seem to be going a bit better for you, that your 'luck' seems to have turned around. That's not a coincidence - that's you, your brain and the Universe working exactly like it should.

So like I said, they don't need to be huge things that you're grateful for. It could be as simple as the 10 minutes extra in bed you had that morning, it might be that your partner brought you a cup of tea in bed, it might be that the sun is shining. It could be that your social media post got more engagement this morning, it could be that someone left you a kind comment or that you've woken up with a bit more clarity and focus on the direction of your business.

Joe Vitale, one of the authors of The Secret among many other books on the Law of Attraction, shared his story of Gratitude in one of his books and it has stuck with me ever since. He was struggling, homeless and living on the streets in Houston. He had nothing on him other than a pencil with an eraser on the end. He had heard about the power of gratitude and feeling pretty helpless at this point decided to give it a go and so looked at the pencil, REALLY looked at it. And he started to think to himself 'I'm grateful for the lead in this pencil'. He realised that the pencil allowed him to write a novel, a love letter, fill in a job application, write a suicide note (a little depressing that one but you get the idea!) He then thought about the eraser on the other end and realised how powerful that was because if he wrote anything he didn't like, he could simply wipe it out and start over.

He says it was focusing on the gratitude of that pencil that opened the door to the Universe, just a crack. He is now a multi-millionaire and prolific bestselling author, speaker and trainer.

And it all started with a pencil.

So imagine what YOU can achieve when you start to express thanks for the things you're grateful for.

'Once you feel grateful, you are in an energy that can create miracles' - Dr Joe Vitale

So how do you express gratitude? Do you have to go out and purchase a pretty butterfly journal in order to show your appreciation?

Absolutely not. You can, for sure. If you're a notebook/stationery kind of girl (I'm a sucker for a new pretty notebook!) and are always looking for an excuse to buy a new notepad or journal then go for it. If that works for you. The most important thing is THAT you do it, not how you do it.

If it feels good for you to be writing down things you're grateful for as soon as you wake up in the morning then go for it.

If you find it easier to note these down just before you go to bed then do that.

If, however, the thought of writing down things you're thankful for every day makes you want to jam your pen in your eye then keeping a Gratitude Journal probably isn't for you.

This doesn't mean that you shouldn't bother with the concept of Gratitude though - there are so many ways you can express things you're thankful for each and every day.

For me, I practice something that I call 'Active Gratitude'. This doesn't involve me writing down my thanks in a journal (though I will do this if I have a specific short term goal I'm working on Manifesting and want to supercharge it) but rather I express gratitude and joy as I'm going about my day.

I'll express thanks to the Universe as I step outside and feel the sun shining down on my face. I'll express thanks for the clear traffic and the parking spaces outside the door of where I'm going (before I even get there), I'll say thank you for the beautiful flowers growing in my garden as I'm sipping my cup of tea and looking out the kitchen windows.

It can feel forced and super cheesy when you first start doing it (especially if you've been a regular complainer like I used to be) but the more you do it the easier and more natural it will feel.

As a reminder, if you REALLY want to create the success you deserve, your gratitude practices - , however you do it - need to be daily.

So start today.

In fact, start right now. Before moving on to the next chapter or getting back to whatever you've got going on today, take 1 minute to share something you're grateful for. You don't even need to write this down if your first thought is 'I haven't got a notebook yet I'll start it tomorrow after I've been to the shops'. Drop the excuses. Unless of course you don't REALLY want to create more success and happiness in your life….

So do it now. Say out loud 'Today I'm grateful for...' and just say the first thing that comes to mind. There's no right or wrong answer here, don't question it or analyse it or wonder whether it's a stupid thing to be thankful for, just go with it.

I'll give you a minute to do this....

Chapter 9

RE-WRITE YOUR STORY

So let's talk about journaling. This is one of those things that's a bit like Marmite - you're either going to love it or hate it (if you're not from the UK and don't know what Marmite is then think about a particular food that has divided your nation...).

If you're already journaling then I assume you love it so that's cool (or you're doing it just because someone has told you to and you have no idea why and feel weird doing it - which is what we'll clear up in this chapter so keep reading).

'Journaling' has become a bit of a buzz word recently with it being thrown around all over social media, from Bullet Journals to Dream Journals to Gratitude Journals....

I get asked frequently whether journaling can actually help with increasing self-confidence and belief and as a result create more success and abundance and my honest answer is this -

ALL the techniques and processes CAN work, it's just whether they work for you. There's no one size fits all with mindset and manifesting and what works for someone else may not work for you. But you'll never know until you try.

Journaling is one of those techniques. Some people will do it every single day, some people will do it when they have a specific goal they want to achieve or a specific limiting belief they want to clear (I fall into this category) and some try it once and never do it again (or never at all).

But with so many people talking about it, there must be a reason - and there is. Journaling is a great way to not only get all of our thoughts out of our head (which brings clarity and calm) but is super helpful for retraining our brain. It's a technique that you can use alongside your Affirmations (which we're going through in the next chapter) to really focus on what you want your Dream Life to look like in order to bring it into your reality much quicker. And as I mentioned a moment ago, you can also use it to get clear on the limiting beliefs, blocks and fears that are holding you back from creating that Dream Life AND write a different story instead.

Which is what we'll focus on in this chapter. Because until you are a little clearer on what your blocks and beliefs are, you won't be able to clear them, you won't be able to face the fear and rise and you won't achieve the level of success you want.

So journaling isn't about keeping a pretty butterfly journal under your mattress, taking it out before bed and writing 'Dear Diary...' then professing your love for the boy who sits two rows behind you in class (was that just me?) - it's about getting your thoughts down on paper. We have so many thoughts a day (like literally tens of thousands) that it's no surprise that sometimes we get a bit overwhelmed, stressed and lose focus. We can't put them into any sort of order or understand where they may be coming from and that's when the fear, the doubt, the anxiety kicks in. A Journal can be a fantastic instrument for 'sorting your thoughts out'.

Do you need to spend lots of money on a pretty journal? Absolutely not. You can get a lovely one from your local pound/discount store I'm sure. Find one that reaches out to you. It may be your favourite colour, it may have a quote on the front that you love, it may simply be a nice hardback notepad that feels smooth to the touch and you have no other reason why you want to pick it up but you do. Of course, if you're a stationary nerd like me then you might want to spend a little more and get the PERFECT one for you, but there really isn't any need. It's more important that the inside of the journal has enough space for you to write, than what the outside looks like.

So what do you write? You can literally write whatever comes to mind. However, you might want to focus on what you're grateful for that day or what you're looking forward to tomorrow. You may want to write your goals and intentions and affirmations. You may just want to use it to braindump everything in your head so you can clearly organise it a bit more.

At the end of this chapter I'm going to give you an exercise you can complete with your journal which will help you get clearer on your limiting beliefs (which you can then use to create some Affirmations in the next chapter) which is a process you can go through every month if you feel the need. A lot of journaling work I find is inspiration. What are you called to write? Remember from Chapter 4 to trust your instincts. Usually your inspiration will guide you to whatever is needed for that day. If you force it, it will feel like a chore, you'll start to resent it and it will actually have a negative effect. If you let inspiration guide you and it's fun for you to do then the benefits will be bountiful.

There have been lots of differing opinions and ideas about WHEN you should actually complete your journaling exercises - some say first thing in the morning, some say last thing at night - but again I would say go with inspiration and whatever works for you. If you're so tired when you go to bed and every night you think 'Oh crap I've got to write my gratitudes in my bloody journal'..... It's probably going to be pretty pointless for you to do. You may as well not bother and just go straight to bed instead. I'm going to go out on a limb and say this probably isn't the best time for you to be journaling.

If first thing in the morning you feel like you're always running around, making the kids lunches while trying to get them to hurry up and put their shoes on so you can get them to school on time and it stresses your tits off to imagine sitting down to write your thoughts down…. Then mornings probably aren't your journaling friend.

Find some time where you can really focus on it. Where you won't have any distractions while you're doing it, when you're calm and relaxed and you can dedicate some time to it. This might mean it's a different time each day. This might mean it's every afternoon for you. Again, go with your intuition here. There is no right or wrong and there is certainly no 'perfect' time to journal - despite what the 'Gurus' say.

Which brings me to my next point. Do you have to do it EVERY day?! Absolutely not. Nope. I don't and you don't have to either. But of course you can. You may find (if you're not already doing it) that you fall in love with the process and the sense of calm and clarity it gives you or the buzz you get from writing down your goals that you want to (i.e. inspired to) do it every day. However, if you're like me, you may just do it when you feel you 'need' to. This may be because you have a particular goal you want to achieve and you want to see what blocks are coming up for you. It may be because you're feeling overwhelmed and want to gain some clarity. Of course, as you know, what you focus on you attract so the more you journal, the quicker it may be for you to see the benefits from it. However, if you don't see yourself as being the 'journal every day' kind of woman then don't stress about it. There are so many other techniques and processes that you can use and this is just one in your arsenal. If you find yourself doing it once a month but don't feel the need to do it any more than that there's probably a reason why. So go with it.

Again, what you really don't want to do is force it. I invested in a course a few years ago, when I was still just getting started on my journey into having a success mindset where the instructor told me to write my affirmation down 55 times in a row. And to do that 5 days in a row. This put me off journaling for another 18 months because my wrist ached and so did my brain. I couldn't see the point in it and it did absolutely nothing for me. I was pissed off with it after the 30th one and forced myself to write it another 25 times. The only thing that happened was I made the decision in that incredibly long 5 days that journaling was a waste of time. That is was something for creative "woo woo" types and certainly not for me. Thankfully I found my way back to it (everything happens for a reason right?) and I realised that it didn't have to be that hard.

Here's a great exercise to get you started. Grab your journal (if you want to get started straight away and you haven't got one yet, just use a piece of paper, that's totally fine). You'll want to find some time where you can be distraction free for at least 15-20 minutes.

Think of a goal that you want to achieve. This might be 'I want more clients for my business' or 'I want to bring in 4k every month' - whatever YOUR goal is that comes to mind.

At the top of the paper write 'I want' and then your goal and then write BUT... at the end.

I.e. 'I want to bring in 4k every month BUT...'

Then just start writing. WHATEVER comes up for you. Don't judge or question or analyse or ask whether that's the right answer, just literally write down every thought that comes to mind once you've written that statement. Write each thought or statement down on a new line and leave a space between (I.e. write on every other line).

This might go a little something like this:

'I want to bring in 4k every month BUT...'

How will I do that? I'm only making 1k a month at the moment.

Is that even possible?

Am I good enough for that?

Do I even want it?

What will my friends think?

Oh I didn't get back to Lisa about Saturday night. What am I going to wear?

It's likely your brain will be going off in different directions and you'll start thinking other unrelated things, just write them down anyway and keep going. If you do find that you've gone off track a bit just read the 'I want BUT...' statement out loud and start writing again.

Keep going until you really can't think of anything else, until it feels forced. Then just stop writing and put your journal aside and leave it for 24 hours (approximately).

You may find that as you continue going about your day after doing this process you'll come up with other doubts and fears and questions. This is because you've sparked the subconscious part of your brain into focusing on that statement and the fears around it and it will continue working even when consciously you've stopped writing. If anything else comes up for you then just add it to your list when you can and put it aside again.

After 24 hours or so I want you to find some distraction free time again to complete this next step.

Grab your journal and go back through your list from the previous day in the following way;

1. Firstly, the only ones you're focusing on now is anything that came up for you in relation to the statement you wrote down (such as 'Am I good

enough for that?' etc). So cross through anything that is unrelated (what am I having for dinner tonight?!).

2. Your next step is to note down after each statement, question or thought whether it is a belief or a fact.

A fact will be something that has been scientifically proven or there can be no other outcome whatsoever. Whereas a belief is something that you believe MAY happen or COULD happen - maybe based on previous experiences - but you do not know for absolute certain.

I.e if you've written down '*It's not possible for me to make 4k a month*' is that a belief or a fact? It's 100% a belief because you do not know without a shadow of a doubt that you can't make 4k a month. Plenty of people make that and more and there is no reason why you can't. Just because you haven't done yet doesn't mean you can't in the future - you see?

So go through each one on your list and note down whether it's a belief or a fact (Hint: I imagine most will be a belief but go with it anyway...). Then move onto the next step.

3. Now you have your list of beliefs and facts - for those that are beliefs, I want you to ask yourself for each one whether it has served you to have this belief. Has it been good for you to believe these thoughts? Has it helped you create the success you desire? Will it help you if you continue to believe this belief? Note down a Yes or a No next to each one.

4. For every one that you decided is a belief that has not or no longer serves you, you're now simply choosing to believe something else. I know it sounds very simple - and it is - but just to be clear this doesn't mean the beliefs you hold are just going to vanish, it's not a magic trick, but implementing this technique and the others that I talk about in this book are pushing your comfort zone, retraining your subconscious and expanding the limitations held within it. So it will cause a ripple effect.

So now grab a fresh page of your journal (or sheet of paper) and for each belief that you had written down previously, you're going to acknowledge it and make the conscious decision to believe something different.

For example: If you had written down '*I'm not good enough to make 4k a month*' and you have decided that is a belief and one that does not serve you, you'll now write down on the fresh sheet '*Thank you brain for trying to keep me safe for giving me the belief that I'm not good enough to make 4k a month, however I no longer choose to believe this and instead I choose to believe that I am more than capable of making 4k a month*'.

Do this for each of your beliefs (this may take some time so you may need to stagger this process over a few days, again, don't force it).

What you'll have once completed is a list of beliefs you're CHOOSING to believe. Read through these daily for the next 14 days to really implant them into your brain.

In the next chapter I'm going to go through Powerful Language and you'll be able to create some Affirmations based on the new beliefs you have established here.

Great work!

Chapter 10

MIND YOUR LANGUAGE

'An Affirmation opens the door. It's a beginning point on the path to change' ~ Louise Hay.

What I share in this chapter has the potential to change your life.

I know what you're thinking. That's quite a bold statement to make.

But I mean every word and I say it from experience. Because it has completely changed mine.

There are so many layers to creating a success mindset and so many individual tools and processes that when you put them together create an ultimate arsenal for your dream life. A super weapon against your fears and doubts and limiting beliefs.

90

But for me, understanding and applying just one in particular allowed me to ditch the law job and fire the boss after 12 years of 'trying' (and allowed my husband to reduce his hours to part time), bring in more money than I ever thought possible and do something that sets my soul on fire.

I'm talking about the power of language.

Because your words mean so much more than you may think.

Everything - and I mean EVERYTHING - that you say is having an effect on your life, your success, your wealth, your health - EVERYTHING.

If you're reading this book and you're not where you want to be (maybe even literally if you're reading this on your lunch break in your crappy job or in your tiny apartment that you want to get out of) then there's a disconnect between what you want and what you say.

Fact.

Remember - (and I know I sound like a stuck record here but I want you to REALLY get it otherwise shit won't change) - what you focus on you attract. This means everything you talk about and how you talk about it you're attracting into your reality.

For example - if you're a serial moaner, finding something to complain about often, you're actually attracting more things to make you complain. Your brain doesn't get that you don't want that stuff, it doesn't understand the negative behind the words, it literally acts on what you tell it.

If I said to you now, whatever you do - DO NOT think of a pink elephant, I DON'T want you to think of a pink elephant at all. What are you now thinking about? More than likely a pink elephant. Because your brain has picked up on the 'thing', i.e. the pink elephant, not on the fact that you're not supposed to think about it, does that make sense?

So just in the same way if you're constantly thinking about how crap your job is, how small your apartment is, how much debt you're in - then your brain will be on the lookout for more of those things (your boss breathing down your neck more than normal, you feel like you're tripping over things in your tiny apartment and more bills land on the doormat). It doesn't understand that you DON'T want those things anymore, basically, if you're talking about it and thinking about it and focusing on it then it assumes you want it. And it always wants to make you happy.

The good news is, it works in the exact opposite way too! So you CAN create the exact level of success you desire, you CAN bring in more money, you CAN leave your job and move home, you CAN clear your debts - by focusing on what you DO want instead.

92

And being really mindful of your language. By that I mean being aware of the things you say and changing your words and phrases where necessary.

I can't stress this enough - this is VITAL if you want to clear those crappy limiting beliefs about you not being good enough and create the life of your dreams.

So how do you know if you're stuck in 'negative speak'? Easy. Review the words you use. This includes whether you're thinking to yourself, speaking out loud to yourself or talking to someone else. Do you find there are certain negative or limiting phrases that you use regularly? (Think back to Chapter 2 - The 7 Year Old Who Rules Your Life).

Do you find yourself thinking or saying things like:

'I'm not good enough for that'
'I can't do that
'I'll never be able to….'
'I wish I wasn't so rubbish at….'
'It's easy for them'
'She's just lucky, it's alright for them but I have to….'

None of the above phrases (and so many more like them) are helping you to clear this crappy belief you're holding about not being good enough.

None of them are filling you with confidence or the motivation to go after what you really want (and deserve).

There's also a good chance that if you've been saying them for so long you think you'll never be able to change but I assure you, you absolutely can. The power of your words is so incredible that you can change your situation pretty quickly. No I'm not talking necessarily overnight (though I did see some changes in my level of positivity and my attitude towards my boss 24 hours after 'giving it a go' when I was first introduced to the idea). But I'm also not talking months or years either.

When you can trick your brain into focusing on something different - and then do this repeatedly - it will do everything in its power to be right. For example, if you start telling yourself 'I am more than good enough to make £5000 a month' when you've only ever brought in £2000 at the most, because your brain acts on what you tell it, it will assume that is true and will be filtering everything around you so that you're basically on the lookout for everything that could bring you that amount of money.

They key word above, however, is REPEATEDLY. If you say out loud once that you're good enough to make £5k a month when for the past 18 years you've been telling yourself that it's not possible for you, there's no way you could even make that amount of money and money is the root of all evil anyway..... Then I'm sorry but that will do bugger all and you might as well not waste the breath. It can take a while to retrain your subconscious brain to believe something new (thereby extending the walls of your comfort zone) and so the more often you can say it the better.

Just to be clear, I'm not saying you have to stand in the mirror 38 times a day shouting the same words over and over to yourself - that will actually have an opposite effect as you'll get so fed up with it. But if you can build up the habit of being really mindful of your language throughout your day it will start to get easier and easier and you'll notice the effects much quicker.

So what should you say instead?

Basically, anything that takes away the doubt or disbelief. In order to grow in confidence you have to talk AS IF you already are. In order to become more successful you have to talk AS IF you already are.

Change all your

'I can't'
'I won't'
'I shouldn't'"
And 'I'll never be able to'

To

'I can'

'I am'

And 'I will'.

'I AM good enough to make £5k per month'

'I WILL smash my targets for this month'

'I CAN achieve the level of success I desire'

This does trip so many people up and causes confusion because you're (more often than not) going to be saying something you don't believe. But remember, you don't believe it because your brain has built up the walls of your comfort zone based on everything you HAVE been saying up until now. If you want to believe new things, you have to tell your brain that you already do. Then, you'll discover after a while that you actually DO believe those things and new limitations will come up for you to work on (it's very unlikely you'll ever be free of limiting beliefs because it's just how your brain works but once you understand - and apply - this concept, you'll have a tool for clearing them and moving forward, clearing and moving forward).

Here's something so you can get started straight away. Remember the 'I want BUT' list you created in the last chapter? With all the negative statements that came up for you? You can now use these to create positive affirmations instead.

What does that mean? An Affirmation is a statement that is said to be true. This means that in mindset terms, it is a statement you can say, as if it already happened, in order to manifest it (manifest just means 'make real' - you bring it into your reality).

For every limiting belief or negative statement or question you wrote down in the exercise in the last chapter, now create a positive Affirmation (statement) around that. This may mean flipping it on its head entirely to turn it from a negative to a positive or it may mean turning a question into a positive declaration.

I.e. If you had written down in the last exercise:

I want to make £4k a month BUT...

I'm not good enough to do that.
How would that even be possible?
Where would the money come from?
I'm no expert, who would even listen to me?

You might then turn these into positive Affirmations like:

'I am more than good enough to make £4k a month every single month'
'At least £4k a month flows to me easily and effortlessly'
'Money flows into my life from a variety of sources every single day'
'I am a powerful leader and my Tribe is growing daily'

Make sure they're in your own words and language so it feels natural to you and make sure they are positive statements, said in the first person as if already happened.

If you want to have more confidence - affirm it.
If you want to feel good enough - affirm it
If you want to increase your income - affirm it.

It is endless the amount of things you can use affirmations for and when you say them enough they will become part of your daily life.

Because the power of Affirmations have had such an impact on my success (both in business and in life), I've talked about it a lot! You can find some further resources at www.thedreamlifecreatorshub.com

It's not all about Affirmations though. Being mindful of your words and language in general will have a huge impact on your confidence and success.

Note when you say 'hopefully' and change it for 'I am' 'I will' or 'I can' (hopefully suggests some doubt in your ability or whether it's possible, which will keep you within the walls of your comfort zone). So *'Hopefully I'll hit my targets this month'* instead becomes *'I WILL hit my targets this month'*.

Get rid of 'one day' and 'someday' because that shit isn't ever going to happen. Your brain loves specificity and one day and someday are too vague and again you're telling your brain that you're not sure if it's possible for you. So *'One day I'll be more successful'* instead becomes *'I AM becoming more and more successful every day!'* Can you see the difference there? Say those two statements out loud now - which one feels better? Which one motivates you more to get off your butt and do something?

This also doesn't stop with just you. Like I mentioned earlier in this chapter, your words are just as important when talking to other people. When you can master this, the doors of opportunity will fly open for you.

Because of our crappy limiting beliefs and the society we're brought up in, we're led to believe that we shouldn't brag about ourselves or be 'too confident' otherwise we'll be labelled as arrogant or cocky. This prevents us from bigging ourselves up when we've done something awesome or talking too passionately and confidently about ourselves, what we're good at and why we deserve it. I've been there too. I've referred to my business as my 'little side business', I've not told people about successes I've had because I worried what they'd think and I was absolutely crap at taking a compliment. Always following it up with 'Oh yeah right, I don't think so!' or 'Thanks for lying but no' etc.

All this did was kept me playing small. The Universe and my brain assumed that because I wasn't shouting from the rooftops about my wins that I didn't actually want them so it stopped me from achieving much more. It picked up on the fact that I referred to my business as my 'side business' so it made sure I never made more money than my salaried job. It noted that every time someone asked me how my business was going I'd respond with 'not bad!' which, although technically this meant it was good it also noted that when I said that, my stomach would turn into knots and I'd be panicking hoping they'd change the subject so I didn't have to admit how shit everything was and that I was a big fat failure.

Once I understood how all this was blocking my potential and I made damn sure to change my language at every opportunity, things REALLY changed.

I was able to leave my Law job just four months after changing my language around my job, my boss and the fact that my business was NOT a side business.

I moved my family and I into our beautiful 3 bedroom home in the country just 8 WEEKS after saying daily 'I am so happy and grateful to live in such a beautiful 3 bedroom home in the country'.

I have made multiple 5 figures within a week just from telling myself - and others - that I will.

My relationship with my husband has improved, my confidence has grown so much that I don't even recognise myself to the scared shitless person I was three years ago, my business has grown, my tribe has grown.

And so much more.

So now it's your turn.

What will you create just by speaking it into reality?

The only limitations are the ones you set upon yourself.

Chapter 11

YOUR PROMISE

So I've given you the tools and techniques and processes within this book that have helped me change MY life and have helped me create more success, feel more positive, more abundant, more joyful and have more income coming in.

But it's not going to work for YOU until you DECIDE that it is. Until you choose right here, right now, today that YOU. ARE. ENOUGH.

Whatever your situation, wherever you are, whatever your circumstances, you are more than good enough. You CAN achieve whatever you want, you CAN create that success, you CAN have the life that you're dreaming of.

So make the promise to yourself today that you're no longer going to let your fears and your limiting beliefs win. You're no longer going to let your brain win. You understand that your brain is keeping you safe, it's doing its job, but you're now choosing to tell it something else. You are NOW creating your destiny. You are now creating your legacy. You can be, do and have whatever you want. No limitations. No doubts. No ifs or buts. You can create that dream life that you've been waiting on, you just need to decide it's possible. You just need to believe that you are good enough and to make the promise to yourself today that you're choosing to love yourself, to believe in yourself, to trust yourself and that today is the day you shift.

Because otherwise what's going to change? Where will you be in five years time? In 10 years or 20 years? Will you look back on your life and ask yourself 'what if'? Will you look back wondering what could have been? Will you look back wishing that you had taken those opportunities, wishing that you'd had just a little more faith, more belief in yourself and the possibilities that were there for you? Will you look back with resentment?

Or will you look back and know that you took the risk, that you grabbed the opportunity by the balls and you ran with it and you CREATED your life. You created the most amazing version of your dream life and you did it for yourself. You did it because you're good enough. You did it because you cared. And you did it because you believed in yourself.

I BELIEVE IN YOU.

Though it doesn't actually matter what anyone else thinks, right? I trust that this message has come across within the pages of this book. What matters is that YOU believe in you.

So I encourage you to make the promise to yourself today, in fact, say it out loud with me now:

'*I promise to believe in myself from this day forward. I am more than good enough and anything is possible for me!*'

Good job!

(If you cheated and didn't actually say it then go back and say it now….I'll wait, no worries ;)).

So you've made this wonderful declaration to yourself that you're now choosing to create your ultimate dream life, so what's next?

Well I want to leave you with one final exercise and this is my most favourite technique that I do regularly whenever I'm working on a new goal, whenever I want to clear the limiting beliefs and whenever I want to remind myself that anything is possible, that my dream life is out there waiting for me.

Grab a journal or a notebook for this (I have a specific one that I use just for this process and you may want to do the same). You're going to want to find some distraction free time to do this. I'd say at least 30 minutes would be good. In this exercise you're going to write down your 'Perfect Day'. This is your absolute, ideal, perfect, dream day.

Write out a journal entry, in the first person ('I wake up, I eat, I go..) from the moment you wake up in the morning to the moment you go to bed at night. As if you're living your perfect day. Almost like you're writing a script for a movie about your dream life and you're the star.

Write down EVERYTHING that makes up your ideal, perfect, dream day. When, where and how do you wake up? Who are you next to when you wake up?! What do you do, what do you eat, what do you wear, where do you go, where are you living and what does your home look like? What car do you drive? (Or in your dream day do you have your own driver?!). Remember THERE ARE NO LIMITATIONS. Anything you desire is possible for you so don't filter, don't write something and then scribble it out because you think it's too big. Write it into existence.

Then when you've got your Perfect Day entry, read it regularly (once a week or more) to remind yourself of it, especially when you are letting those limiting beliefs and those fears and doubts take over (which is normal remember). Remind yourself of what it is that you're working towards. Remind yourself that your dream life is already out there waiting for you.

Speak it into existence. Grab it by the balls. And go get it!

Chapter 12

DOING IT FOR THE KIDS

When my daughter was two years old she told me that she was going to be a Superhero when she grows up.....

No laughing, no jokes, she was absolutely positively serious. She was going to be a Superhero.

She can and she will.

(At the time of writing she no longer wants to be a Superhero, she's now four and wants to be a Paleontologist but I'm sure that may change again by the time this book is printed...)

I imagine we all had beliefs like that when we were young. I wanted to be a Foreign Correspondent, mixing my love of writing with my enjoyment of learning languages and Spanish being my favourite class in High School because of my awesome teacher Mrs. Rosa. Until I didn't quite get the grade I wanted (which was still a very good grade now that I look back on it) so decided I was useless and not cut out to do that, it would be too hard, I'd probably fail so might as well not bother.

What did you want to be? Are you doing that now? If not, why not? (Ok, I get that it may not actually be possible for you to be a Superhero…..but did you not go after something because you decided you wouldn't be able to? It would be too hard? You weren't good enough for it?)

Now that I know what I know about our brains, our beliefs and how they're formed at such a young age, I'm so careful of what I say, how I say it and how I act around my daughter. I know that she'll still have some limitations and doubts because, again, that's just how our brains work. But I DO NOT want to be the reason that she doubts herself. I DO NOT want to be the reason she doesn't go after her dreams. I DO NOT want to be the reason that she takes a mundane job that sucks her soul just because she feels she should. I want her to know that anything is possible if she sets her mind to it. From digging up fossils and studying them to rescuing people using her super powers.

I want her to know that she can be, do and have anything she wants. I want her to have the most amazing, extraordinary, phenomenal life.

And in order for that to be possible I had to make the change for ME first. To be an inspiration and a positive example in her life.

And I know it's working. A few months ago she was colouring and was trying to stay in the lines, when she made a mistake she threw her crayon down and said 'I can't do it!' But very quickly she corrected herself and said 'No, stand up tall, stand up straight and say I BELIEVE IN ME'. Then picked up her crayon and carried on with her task. At four years old. My heart almost exploded with pride.

So after everything I've shown you in this book, if you're still doubting whether it's possible, if you're still questioning whether it can actually make a difference, if you're thinking it's been a good book but you probably won't put much into action......

Then I implore you. If not for you, will you join me in doing it for the kids?

The leaders of the next generation. The Presidents, the CEOs, the Teachers, the Scientists, the Astronauts, the Explorers, the Paleontologists and the Super Heroes. More importantly - the HAPPY, confident ones.

The changes you make today will have a ripple effect for generations.

Would you rather leave them a legacy of limitations?

The choice is yours.

About Gemma

Gemma is a Law of Attraction and Success Mindset Trainer, Speaker, Coach and Author helping female entrepreneurs create the life of their dreams with Practical Woo.

Long story short, she used to live in a place of scarcity and lack. Then she learnt some awesome things about the power of our brains, our language and our mindset and it is now her passion to help others create their dream life and live out the best version of themselves, by breaking through their barriers and limitations, to change what is possible with powerful language (that's kind of her super power…) and to live happier, wealthier and more abundantly in all aspects.

She dreamed of being an author since she was old enough to hold a pen and she's grateful that not only has one of her own dreams now been fulfilled, but she also gets to impact the world with her books so that others can create their dreams too.

Stay Connected with Gemma

Resources: www.thedreamlifecreatorshub.com

Facebook: https://www.facebook.com/DreamLifeCreators

Free Community 'The Dream Life Creators Club':

https://www.facebook.com/groups/SuperManifesters/

Pinterest: https://www.pinterest.co.uk/DreamLifeCreators/

Printed in Great Britain
by Amazon

40220498R00068